MW01634042

Soul of Rome

A GUIDE TO EXCEPTIONAL EXPERIENCES

WRITTEN BY CAROLINA VINCENTI
PHOTOGRAPHED BY SOFIA BERNARDINI AND CLAIRE DE VIRIEU
ILLUSTRATED BY CLARA MARI

JONGLEZ PUBLISHING

Travel guides

‘*THERE IS ONLY ONE ROME
IN THE WORLD. HERE I FEEL
LIKE A FISH IN WATER …*’

GOETHE

Rome: Travel instructions

Taking on Rome is no easy task: there are too many layers, too much history, too many monuments. Rome, the Eternal City by definition, eludes any simple attempts at classification; there are so many (too many) stories, images, tales. That's why we created this guide through a process of elimination, choosing only those fragments of the city's soul that, in our opinion, have resisted the uniformity of globalisation and mass tourism. At the same time, how can anything remain secret in a place that has been explored for centuries? So, starting from the premise that no other metropolis has played such a central role in history over the last 2,500 years, we sifted through the present in search of traces of character that have crystallised in the city's spaces. In writing about them, we let ourselves be guided by our hearts, avoiding simply compiling a list of addresses.

Rome used to be where you went to forge an education by exposing yourself to the experiences of life and knowledge that we call culture. Pilgrims sought the soul of the place in the sacred, while laymen sought it in the profane; but both went into raptures about the stones, churches and palaces.

Yet, in reality, the soul of Rome, then as now, is to be found in its contradictions. A popular and patrician city, forever bountiful and generous: like the colonnade of St Peter's welcoming children in its embrace; the meanderings of the Tiber encircling the domes of the historic centre; and the narrow winding streets preceding the oval of Piazza Navona, the city's Baroque lounge. A 'magical and poisonous city' (in the words of poet Valerio Magrelli), it continues to offer itself to us in all its greatness and decadence. A place of idleness *par excellence*; an idleness extolled by the ancients, as it happens.

What we have tried to do is write about the experiences you can have in its streets and alleyways, strolling Roman-style, allowing yourself to be blinded by the sun on its terraces, or abandoning yourself to the pleasures of its cafés, where Romans read the papers with the nonchalance of those who have lived through so many centuries and know that everything passes.

The Romans have every cuisine in the world at their fingertips yet they prefer to surrender to the joys of *pasta carbonara* in a dark alley, or *grattachecca* (ice shaved from a block on demand and flavoured with pieces of fresh fruit) from a kiosk on the banks of the Tiber, just like a hundred years ago.

We like to think that the places in our guide will strike a chord with travellers, allowing them to gather fragments of authentic Roman life from these small islands where the city's ancient and future soul is still offered up for the taking.

Carolina Vincenti

WHAT YOU WON'T FIND
IN THIS GUIDE

- directions to the Colosseum
- hop-on hop-off open-top bus stops
- touristy trattorias near the Trevi Fountain

WHAT YOU WILL FIND
IN THIS GUIDE

- aphrodisiacal *pasta carbonara*
- where to enjoy a glass of wine on the street, surrounded by locals
- how to sleep in a cardinal's bed
- rare herbs from the Roman countryside
- Caravaggio's barber
- the Vatican Museums before the crowds get there
- the world's oldest road you can cycle along
- the pope's socks

THE SYMBOLS OF
SOUL OF ROME

Less
than €10

€10
to €40

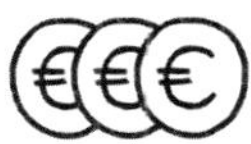

More
than €50

First come,
first served

Make
a reservation

100%
Roman

Opening times often vary,
so we recommend checking them directly
on the website of the place you plan to visit.

30 EXPERIENCES

01. Go bargain-hunting at the amateur flea market
02. The barber of Caravaggio
03. An underground venue in a military fort
04. Spend a night in the most beautiful villa in Rome
05. Traditional Roman cuisine with a creative twist
06. Discover contemporary Roman cooking
07. On the quest for Rome's best ice cream
08. Escape the crowds in an exceptional palace
09. The ultimate espresso
10. Buy socks like the pope's
11. A rooftop straight out of a dream
12. Chilling on the street with a glass of wine in your hand
13. Roman-style street food in Campo de' Fiori
14. A musical soirée in a secret chapel
15. Have dinner at a deli
16. High-quality Roman cuisine in a low-key location
17. Buy groceries direct from the best local farmers
18. Italian songs in a park with breathtaking views
19. Talking to angels in the Basilica of Santi Quattro Coronati
20. Go for a ride on the oldest road in the world
21. The best pizza in Rome
22. Visit one of Rome's most magical places without the crowds
23. A biscuit that will take you back in time
24. Like a Sunday in the country
25. A great little bistro in a fishmonger's shop
26. Visiting the Vatican without tourists
27. The privilege of visiting the most private villa
28. Rome's loveliest libraries
29. Jogging among the gods of the stadium
30. Visit one of the most beautiful villas in Italy

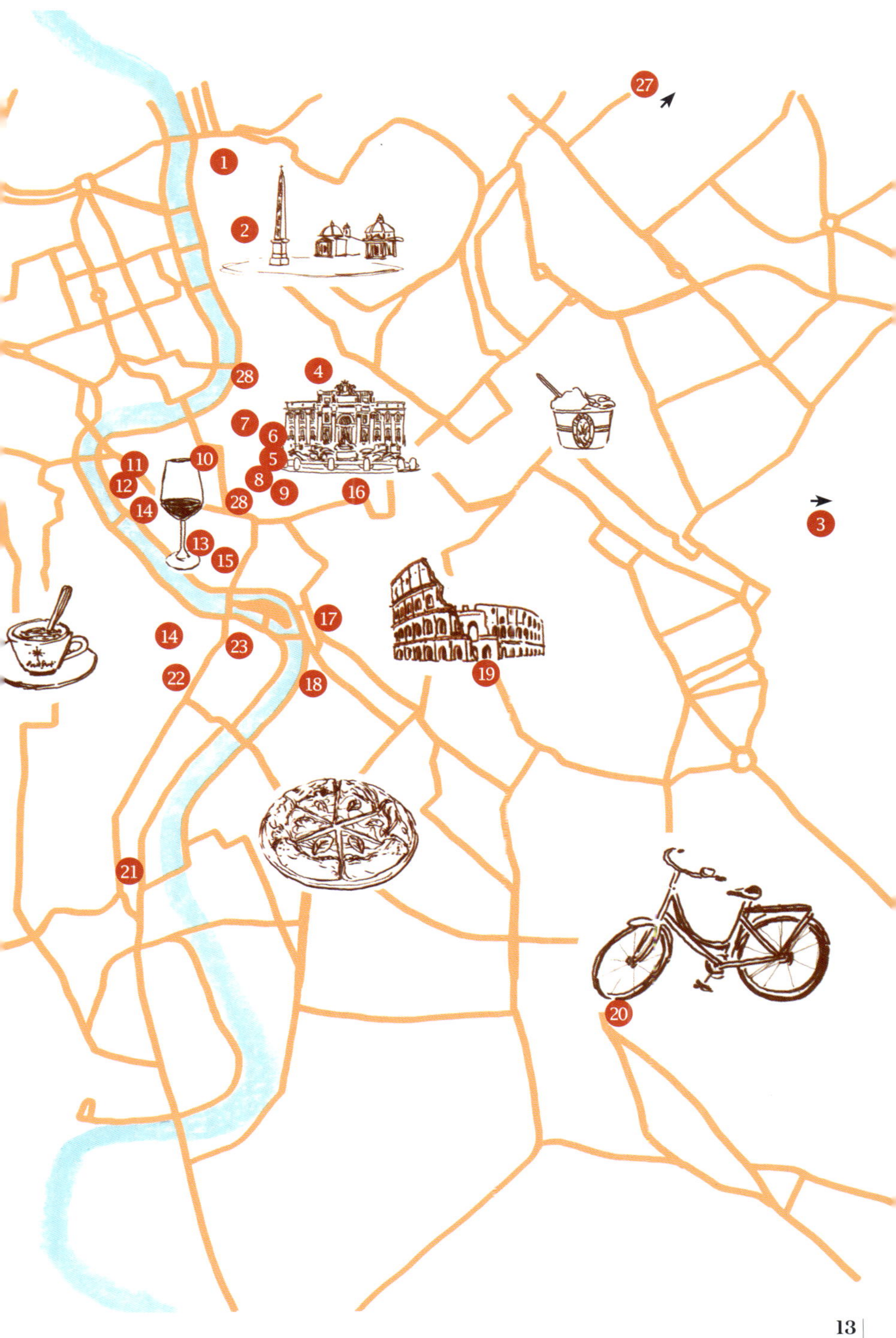

1
2
27
28
4
7
6
5
10
11
12
14
8
28
9
16
3
13
15
14
17
23
22
18
19
21
20

GO BARGAIN-HUNTING AT THE AMATEUR FLEA MARKET

It's a real pleasure to wander around the flea market of Borghetto Flaminio (also called the Rigattieri per Hobby – *rigattiere* means 'second-hand goods dealer'), just a few steps from Piazza del Popolo. This is where, every Sunday, after having gone through their wardrobes during the week, the capital's upper-middle class rent a table to sell the clothes they no longer wear.

You'll find a whole lot of vintage items and sometimes luxury brands (ties, handbags and even table linen, sheets or cufflinks) in a friendly and rather 'hobbyist' atmosphere.

Over the years, the two owners, Paolo Tinarelli and Enrico Quinto, have amassed one of the richest collections of Italian clothes from the late 1950s – they breathe new life into them by taking them on travelling exhibitions around the world.

The beautiful National Etruscan Museum of Villa Giulia is just a stone's throw away.

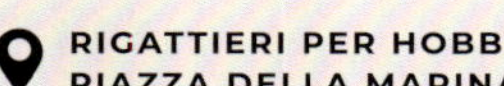

RIGATTIERI PER HOBBY
PIAZZA DELLA MARINA 32

+39 06 5880 517
mercatidiroma.com/pulci/borghetto-flaminio

SUN: 10am / 7pm

THE BARBER
OF CARAVAGGIO

Rome has as many barbers as a Rossini opera, but some are more special than others, including these two:

> SALA DA BARBA GENCO

It's said that at the foot of the Torre della Scimmia, Caravaggio, who lived nearby, got into a fight with a barber boy. The place still exists; Sala da Barba Genco is now the city's oldest barbershop. In addition to classic cuts, Roberto, the nephew of founder Silvano Rossi, offers his 'Genco shave' – 50 delightful minutes, involving rose water, argan oil, calendula cream, and more.

**SALA DA BARBA GENCO
VIA DEI PORTOGHESI 17**

+39 06 686 9881

gencosaladabarba.com

BARBIERE
17

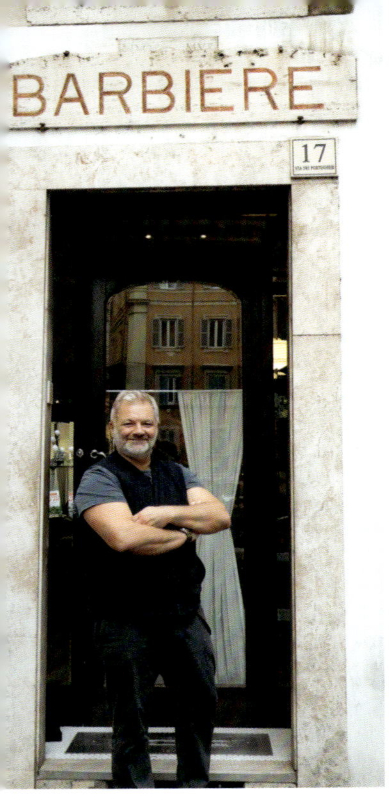

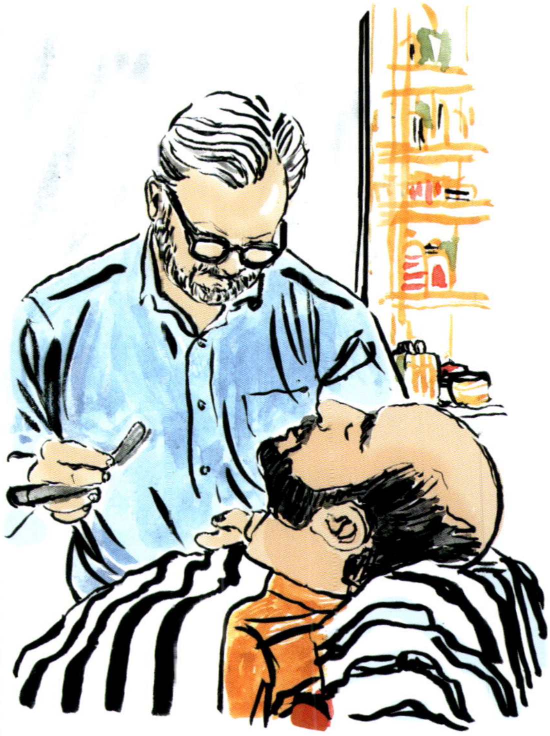

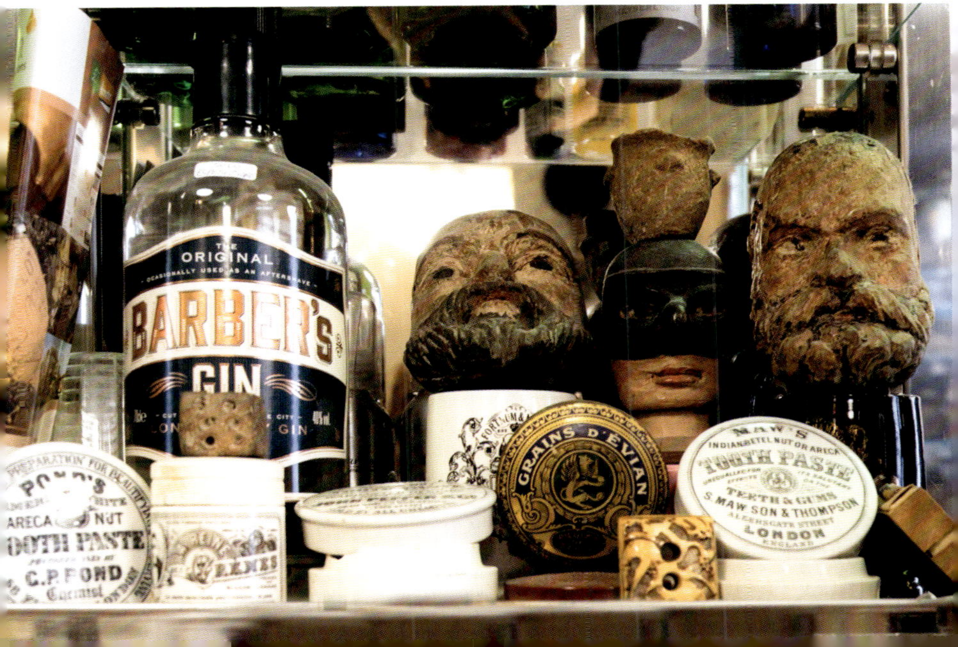
THE ORIGINAL
OCCASIONALLY USED AS AN AFTERSHAVE
BARBER'S
GIN
GRAINS D'EVIAN
MAW'S
TOOTH PASTE
TEETH & GUMS
S. MAW SON & THOMPSON
LONDON
ARECA NUT
TOOTH PASTE

For those who speak Italian, Giuseppe Cerroni can take you on a true journey back in time to the golden years of Cinecittà. After starting out as an apprentice to Dino De Laurentiis's barber, and as Silvana Mangano's hairstylist, he went on to style the hair of most of the actors and directors of the 1960s: Ferreri, Comencini, Guttuso, Pasolini and Moravia, who wouldn't devote more than four minutes to his beard while Elsa Morante waited impatiently for him …

What has stayed with Giuseppe from those years are endless anecdotes and an inimitable know-how. His speciality is a scalp massage, ideally rounded off with hand (up to the elbow) and foot (up to the knee) treatment.

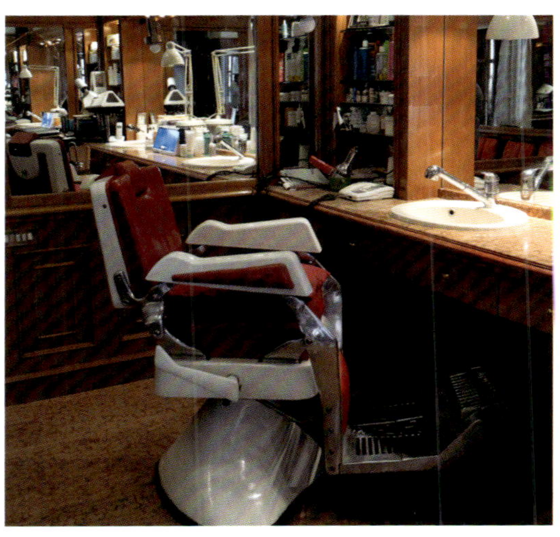

 **GIUSEPPE CERRONI ACCONCIATORE**
VIA GIAMBATTISTA VICO 44

+39 06 361 1465

AN UNDERGROUND VENUE
IN A MILITARY FORT

Tucked away in a public park in the eastern suburbs of Rome, the former military fort Prenestino, built in the late 19th century, has transformed into one of the most exciting underground venues in the city.

Spanning 13 hectares, it offers a vast array of activities day and night: exhibitions, film and documentary screenings, parties, concerts, theatre performances, a tea room, a pub and a variety of classes, including music, languages, boxing, karate, kung fu, yoga, Pilates, Qigong, pole dancing, salsa and tango. There are also workshops in crafts, botany and cycling.

Don't miss out!

FORTE PRENESTINO
QUARTIERE PRENESTINO-CENTOCELLE
VIA FEDERICO DELPINO / VIA EMILIO CHIOVENDA

forteprenestino.net

From Termini station: trams 5 and 19

AREA BIMBI
PALCO
OFFICINE NATURALI
TEATRO FORTE

I ♥ XM24

- VALERIO MAGRELLI -

POET

Is Rome still poetic?

Yes, in spite of itself. Sometimes I'm amazed when I notice certain buildings or certain streets where the city's millennial stratification is powerfully revealed. I ask myself how it's possible that so many different people managed to create so much beauty without consulting with each other. In Rome, the urban planning sometimes seems to have developed entirely on its own, in a coherent and necessary manner, as autonomously as a botanical miracle.

Where else do you still see traces of the soul of the city?

It's pointless to give in to nostalgia, but of course it's still lovely when you happen on an artisanal boutique that has survived the tidal wave of Irish pubs and Bengali catch-all shops. While Rome's historical problem lies in its management, it's surprising to discover places or practices that are managing to resist the brutal commercialisation that came to a head with a chariot-racing project at Circus Maximus. You might as well just bring the lions back to the Colosseum, as long as you replace the ancient Christians with the current administrators.

A poetic motto?

'Magical and poisonous', a definition of Rome taken from the travel diary of Jean-Paul Sartre that seems to me to sum up perfectly the feeling of a millennia-old metropolis as sublime as it is detestable. Not many have expressed so succinctly the oxymoronic, contradictory, irremediable nature that contrasts the sublime vertigo of the city's places with a population oppressed by centuries of theocracy. I don't think anyone can hate the Romans more than someone who was born in Rome.

Which poetic text about the city do you think deserves to be better known?

Italy has a tremendous poet who isn't well known at all, even though he was admired by contemporaries of his such as Goethe and Stendhal: Giuseppe Gioachino Belli, whose sonnets are absolute 19th-century masterpieces. Belli represents a poet world – perhaps the only one who was capable of merging so absolutely with the beloved-hated city that accommodated him; a material and metaphysical poet who is most similar to the English poet John Donne.

SPEND A NIGHT
IN THE MOST BEAUTIFUL
VILLA IN ROME

It's one of Rome's most amazing secrets. The exquisite Villa Medici offers the privilege of staying in two historic suites which were apartments of the Medici family.

When we say privilege, we mean it: after dinner, as you enter the villa through the small door cut into the large central doorway, you immediately feel you're experiencing something exceptional.

In the silence of the night, go up the villa's wide travertine stairs to the famous gardens.

FOTOS: FRANÇOIS HALARD

 **VILLA MEDICI**
VIALE DELLA TRINITÀ DEI MONTI

Reservations by e-mail only and no more than four months in advance: standard@villamedici.it

Specify that you wish to stay in a historic room (classic rooms, also located in the villa, are available at considerably lower rates)

The two rooms (some 70 square metres – each!) feature 16th-century frescoes by Jacopo Zucchi and coffered period ceilings. They either offer views of the marvellous gardens or 180-degree views of Rome. In the beautiful Salon Lili Boulanger, in front of one of the bedrooms, there's a piano. In 2023, the guest rooms and the Boulanger Salon, along with three other historic rooms of the Villa Medici, were given a modern touch by designer India Mahdavi.

NB: These rooms don't come with luxury-hotel amenities or services: there's no elevator or staff to carry your luggage, and breakfast isn't served. But the experience is unforgettable …

TRADITIONAL ROMAN CUISINE
WITH A CREATIVE TWIST

You're in the heart of the tourist centre but want to avoid the usual scams? Just a stone's throw from the Pantheon, in a picturesque little square in the historic centre, Grano is a very pleasant restaurant that serves the great traditional Roman dishes – *pasta alla carbonara*, *aglio e olio* and *all'amatriciana*, for example – but with a welcome creative twist to switch things up a bit.

The owners, Danilo Frisone and Saverio Crescente, also run Cresci, a restaurant with a small bakery not far from St Peter's Basilica, which supplies Grano with its excellent bread. Two safe bets, both in areas generally overrun with tourists.

PHOTO CREDIT: EMANUELA RIZZO

GRANO
PIAZZA RONDANINI 53

+39 06 6819 2096
ristorantegrano.it

CRESCI
VIA ALCIDE DE GASPERI 11–17

+39 06 5184 2654
cresciroma.it

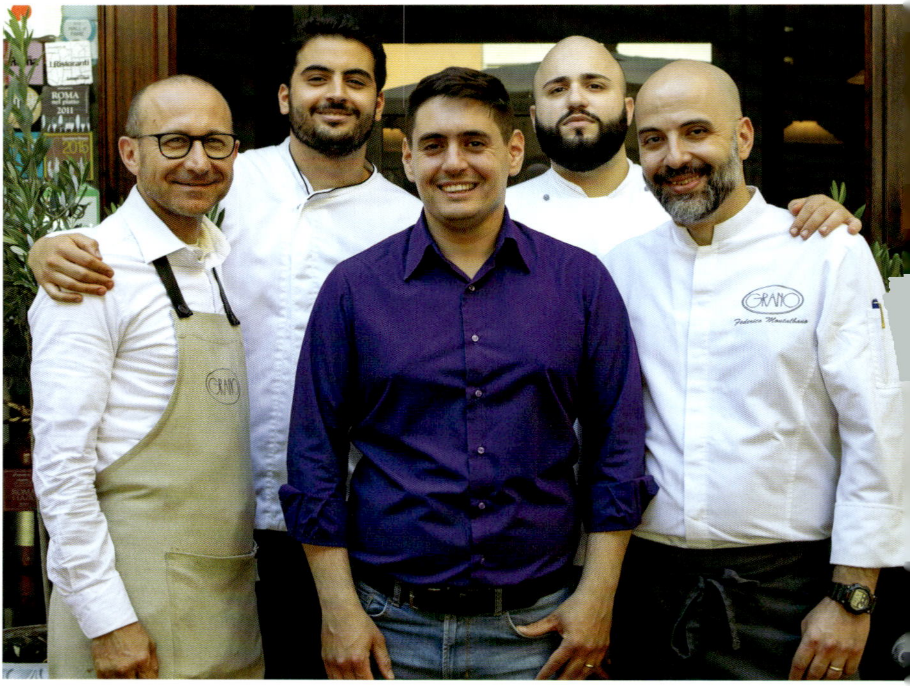
GRANO
Federico Montalbano

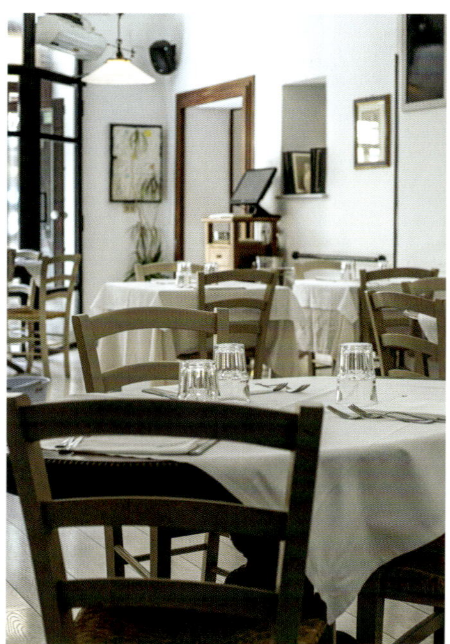

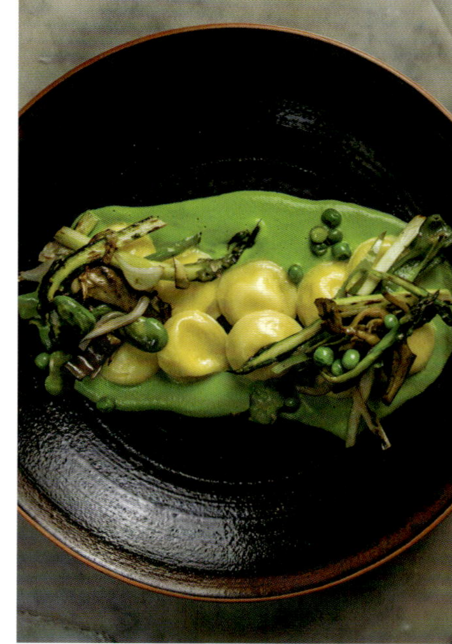

GRANO

DISCOVER
CONTEMPORARY ROMAN COOKING

In its stylish contemporary decor, Retrobottega offers high-quality cooking that relies almost obsessively on the irreproachable quality of its ingredients. Prepared right before the customer, the dishes change each week.

Near the counter demarcating the open kitchen are two convivial tables, each for ten people.

P.S: Retrobottega also has a special pasta workshop and a bar with wines from small producers. Here, once a week, you can eat wild salads foraged by the staff in the Roman countryside, and other goodies.

PHOTO CREDIT: RETROBOTTEGA

RETROBOTTEGA
VIA DELLA STELLETTA 4

retro-bottega.com

Pasta workshop: Retropasta
Via della Stelletta 4
+39 06 6813 6310

Wine bar: Enoteca Retrovino
Via d'Ascanio 26/A

PASTA

ON THE QUEST FOR
ROME'S BEST ICE CREAM

Don't be fooled: in Rome, long waiting lines are not always a guarantee of quality. To find the best ice cream in town, follow this simple advice: for chocolate meringue ice cream and fruit sorbets, trust San Crispino; for the best tiramisu and chocolate flavours, try the Gelateria del Teatro; and for pistachio, Otaleg (that's *gelato* – 'ice cream' in Italian – backwards) and Günther Gelato Italiano are safe bets..

For a seat outside, head over to Pica (the rice pudding and wild strawberry ice creams are superb!) and Palazzo del Freddo, located behind Piazza Vittorio, with its stunning 1930s decor.

<table>
<tr><td>

**GELATERIA
DI SAN CRISPINO**

**Via della Panetteria 42
Piazza della Maddalena 3**
ilgelatodisancrispino.it

</td><td>

**GÜNTHER GELATO
ITALIANO**

Via dei Pettinari, 43
gunthergelatoitaliano.com

</td></tr>
<tr><td>

GELATERIA DEL TEATRO

Via dei Coronari 66
gelateriadelteatro.it

</td><td>

OTALEG

Via di S. Cosimato 14/A
otaleg.com

</td></tr>
<tr><td>

**PALAZZO DEL FREDDO
GIOVANNI FASSI**

Via Principe Eugenio 65
gelateriafassi.com

</td><td>

GELATERIA ALBERTO PICA

Via della Seggiola 12
alberto.pica@hotmail.it

</td></tr>
</table>

ESCAPE THE CROWDS
IN AN EXCEPTIONAL PALACE

When the crowds in the streets, on the piazzas and in the churches and restaurants of Rome are a little too overwhelming, there is a solution for those who cherish silence and tranquillity: the fantastic Altemps Palace located right in the heart of the city.

Interestingly, although the palace and its collections are truly exceptional, the palace itself is empty most of the time.

Wander joyfully among the antique statues up to the beautiful loggia on the first floor. Make sure not to miss the Grande Ludovisi sarcophagus (3rd century AD).

PALAZZO ALTEMPS
PIAZZA DI SANT'APOLLINARE 46

museonazionaleromano.beniculturali.it   Entrance fee: €10

Sant'Eustachio

il caffè

THE ULTIMATE
ESPRESSO

OK, so it's not exactly a secret. But if you're hankering after the ultimate espresso, then head over to Caffè Sant'Eustachio, right around the corner from the Pantheon.

You might have to wait in line, but, while you do, watch the baristas in action behind the coffee machine. You'll probably notice that their hands are hidden by a barrier the technique used to prepare Caffè Sant'Eustachio's speciality, *doppio cremoso* (double creamy), is in fact a secret. Don't worry though – *'cremoso'* doesn't mean there's any milk or cream involved; this espresso is simply so exceptional that it's almost like cream of coffee …

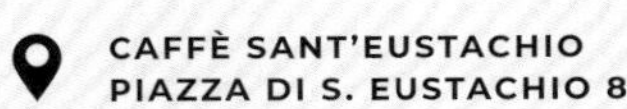

CAFFÈ SANT'EUSTACHIO
PIAZZA DI S. EUSTACHIO 82

+39 06 6880 2048   santeustachioilcaffe.it

A GUIDE TO
COFFEE-DRINKING IN ROME

Cappuccino

CAPPUCCINO: coffee blended
with frothy steamed milk.
Italians drink it at breakfast
or in the course of the morning
but never after meals.

Caffè al vetro

CAFFÈ AL VETRO: espresso serve
in a glass so you can also
appreciate its colour.

Caffè ristretto

CAFFÈ RISTRETTO: a more
concentrated espresso
made with less water.

Granita

GRANITA: a Sicilian recipe
made with coffee and half-crystallised
ice topped with whipped cream.
Perfect for summer.

Macchiato

MACCHIATO: espresso
with a touch
of cold milk foam.

Corretto

CORRETTO: espresso infused
with a small shot
of *grappa* or *sambuca*.

Caffè schiumato

CAFFÈ SCHIUMATO: espresso
capped with a dollop
of hot milk foam.

BUY SOCKS LIKE
THE POPE'S

Founded in the 1790s, Gammarelli has been famous in Rome since 1798. For six generations, Gammare li – and Gammarelli alone – has been dressing the pope.

In addition to cassocks and other clothing reserved for the clergy, Gammarelli also sells exceptional socks, coloured for maximum impact.

So there really is nothing to discuss; simply ask them to open the sock drawers for you so you can choose a crimson or bright red pair ... and nothing else, just like the pope. They're perfect for wearing discreetly (or not) at home, or as a gift for very select friends.

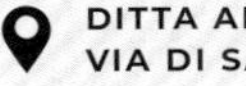 **DITTA ANNIBALE GAMMARELLI
VIA DI SANTA CHIARA 34**

+39 06 6880 1314

gammarelli.com

AMMARELLI
SARTORIA PER ECCLESIASTICI

A ROOFTOP
STRAIGHT OUT OF A DREAM

It's worth making a reservation to secure your spot on Rome's most gorgeous rooftop. From here – the fifth floor of Palazzo Doria Pamphilj, over the library of Pope Innocent X – the view of Piazza Navona, Borromini's Church of Sant'Agnese in Agone just a few metres away, and the rooftops of Rome in general is truly exceptional.

NB: The restaurant's prices – in keeping with the location – are sky-high.

TERRAZZA BORROMINI
VIA DI SANTA MARIA DELL'ANIMA 30

+39 06 6821 5459
+39 391 311 4523

terrazzaborromini.com/contatti

CHILLING
ON THE STREET
WITH A GLASS OF WINE
IN YOUR HAND

Il Goccetto, run by Sergio Ceccarelli – or Sergetto, as everyone calls him – is a mere stone's throw from the Farnese Palace. What makes it truly magical is that you can just take your glass of wine out with you onto the street. Which almost everyone does, since you're not likely to find any room inside …

Then just set down your cheese and meat platter on the bonnet of a parked car and strike up a conversation with your neighbours. The night is off to a good start.

IL GOCCETTO
VIA DEI BANCHI VECCHI 14

+ 39 06 9944 8583

facebook: Ilgoccetto
ilgoccetto@tiscali.it

VINO OLIO
Enoteca
Il Goccetto

ROMAN-STYLE STREET FOOD
IN CAMPO DE' FIORI

It isn't easy to figure out where to have lunch in the uber-touristy Campo de' Fiori without falling into a tourist trap.

Head over to the south-west corner of the square to Forno di Campo de' Fiori for some delectable *pizza rossa* (red pizza). Not really pizza at all, except in name (and dough), *pizza rossa* is a sort of sandwich with tomato sauce that you eat standing up, just like the locals – who flock to this Roman institution no less than tourists do.

Another pro: *pizza rossa* will set you back less than €1.50.

If you're really hungry and want to switch up your palate, try the *pizza bianca* (white pizza), which is available filled with mortadella, among other options.

 **FORNO DI CAMPO DE' FIORI**
PIAZZA CAMPO DE' FIORI 22

+39 06 6880 6662

fornocampodefiori.com

BURTON
Forno
dé Fiori
1880
Forno
Campo dé Fiori
dal 1880

A MUSICAL SOIRÉE
IN A SECRET CHAPEL

Hidden away at the end of one of the many streets that run perpendicular to Via Giulia, the Oratorio del Gonfalone is a small 16th-century marvel. The stunning interior is covered entirely with an extraordinary cycle of frescoes depicting the Passion of Christ in twelve episodes, painted in 1573.

The wooden ceiling carved by Ambrogio Bonazzini in 1568 is also remarkable. The best way to visit this little-known gem is by going to one of the classical music soirées held here almost every Thursday evening from mid-October to the end of May.

The word *gonfalone*, which means 'banner or 'flag', refers to the fact that, in the 14th century, the members of the brotherhood that owned the oratory used to carry the banner of the pope, who was in Avignon at the time, in support of his role as ruler of Rome.

 **ORATORIO DEL GONFALONE**
VIA DEL GONFALONE 32/A

oratoriogonfalone.eu

info@oratoriogonfalone.eu
oratoriodelgonfalone@libero.it

HAVE DINNER
AT A DELI

Just around the corner from Campo de' Fiori, with a decor that's a perfect cross between deli and trattoria, Roscioli is an obligatory stop for anyone exploring the flavours of Roman cuisine.

Using premium ingredients, Roscioli executes all traditional Italian and Roman dishes to perfection, including the famous *cacio e pepe* (pasta with cheese and pepper) and the even more renowned *pasta carbonara*: pasta, pecorino, a mix of exotic peppers, a touch of magic, and that's it.

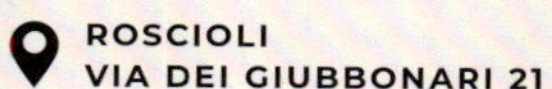

ROSCIOLI
VIA DEI GIUBBONARI 21

+39 06 687 5287

info@salumeriaroscioli.com
salumeriaroscioli.com

€58,00
€28,00
€58
BHRUT   58,00
PBPBUN   58,00
ASANS   95,00
ASWARASOLA   36,00

LA PIGNA

HIGH-QUALITY
ROMAN CUISINE
IN A LOW-KEY LOCATION

Just a stone's throw from the crowds around the Pantheon, La Pigna is a little miracle of calm and the only restaurant on the lovely Piazza della Pigna. Head here for first-rate Roman cuisine, such as the excellent *mezzo rigatone all'amatriciana*, *tonnarello cacio e pepe*, roast beef or braised beef cheek.

PHOTO CREDIT: TRATTORIA PIGNA

LA PIGNA
PIAZZA DELLA PIGNA 54

+39 06 678 5555

lapignaroma.it

BUY GROCERIES DIRECT
FROM THE BEST
LOCAL FARMERS

Taking our cue from the Romans, who know how it's done, we do our grocery shopping at the stalls in this convivial covered market just a stone's throw from the Circus Maximus and the Forum.

Every weekend, producers from the Roman countryside come into town to sell forgotten herbs, wild asparagus, freshly pressed olive oil, Roman chicory, winter artichokes and ancient varieties of fruit. At the back, in the open courtyard with a view of the historic centre, you can also sample dishes prepared in a friendly, down-to-earth atmosphere.

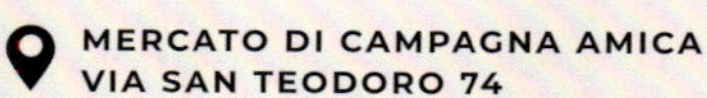

MERCATO DI CAMPAGNA AMICA
VIA SAN TEODORO 74

mercatocircomassimo.campagnamica.it
mercatocircomassimo@campagnamica.it
Instagram: @campagna_amica_circomassimo

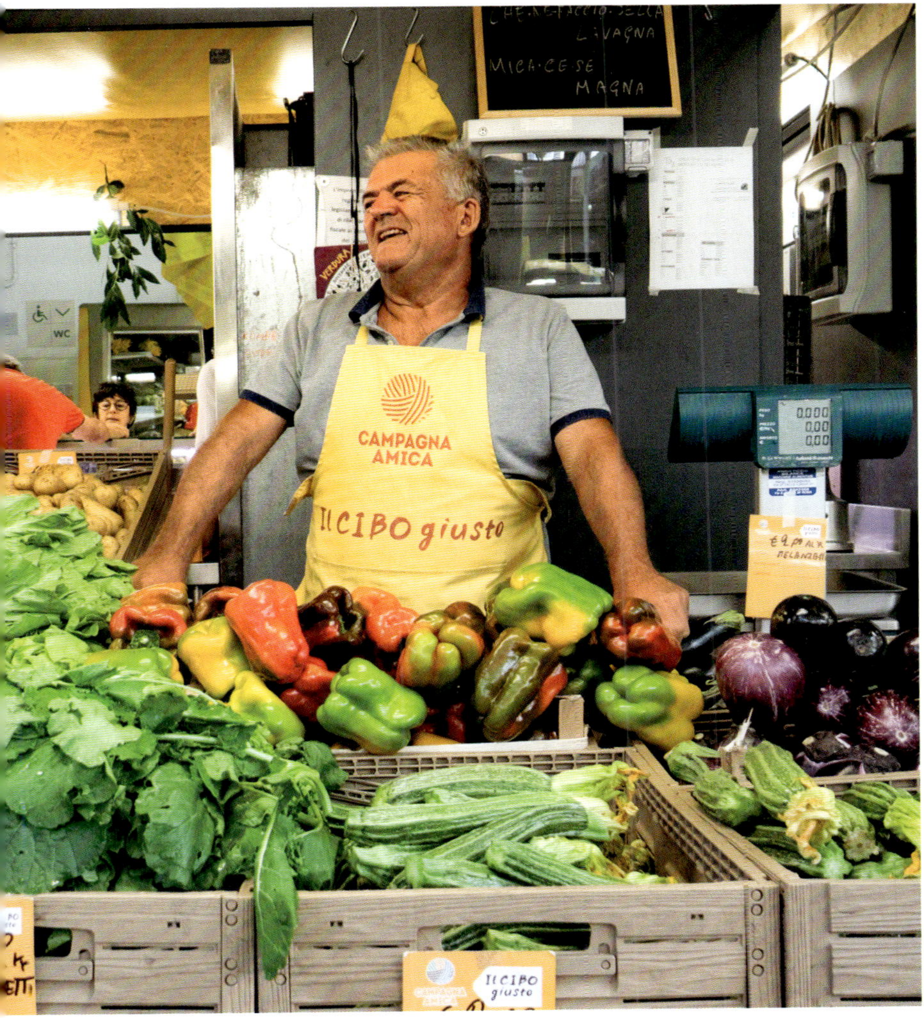
LAVAGNA
MICA CE SE
MAGNA
CAMPAGNA
AMICA
Il CIBO giusto
Il CIBO
giusto

MERCATO
AMICO

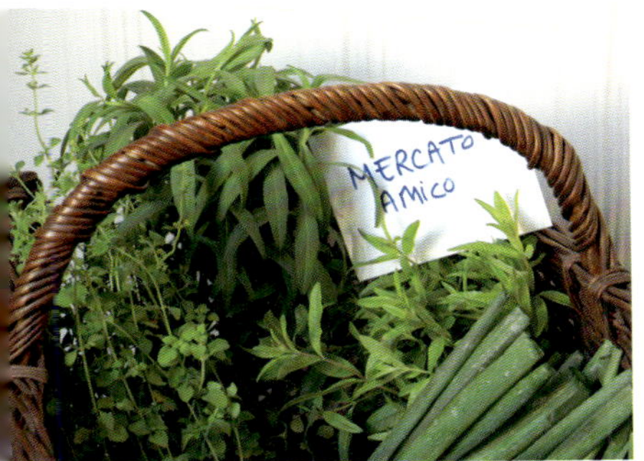

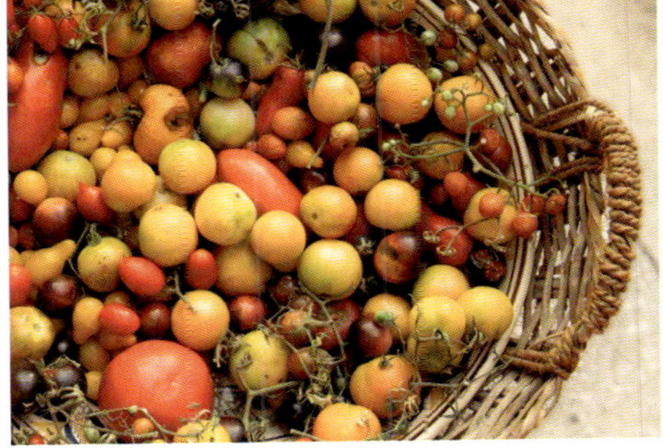

Frutti Mix Frutta
Pomodori
Pere
Prodotti coltivati,
selezionati ed essiccati
direttamente da noi,
senza aggiunta
di sale, zuccheri e
...nti ...
snack
Via Campo
SEZZE SCA
Cell. 347.1

OFFERTA
RAPE ROSSE
€ 1,50 AL MZ
OFFERTA
MELONE RETATO SPACCARELLO
€ 1,00 KG
€ 1,20 L'ETTO
INS. TAGLIO
VALERIANA
€ 0,80 L'UNO
RAVANELLI
€ 2,50 AL K.
PEPERONI FRIGITELLI
€ 4,90 AL K.
CICORIA CAMPO PULITA
€ 2,50 AL K.
PEPERONI
€ 5,90 AL K.
FAGIOLINI BOBY
€ 1,90 AL K.
MELANZANE MISTE
€ 2,90 AL K.
ZUCCHINE ROTANESCHE
€ 1,90 AL K.
ZUCCHINE
€ 1,50 AL K.
CAROTE MAZZI
PERE COSCIA
TOMATO CILIEGINO

ITALIAN SONGS
IN A PARK WITH BREATHTAKING VIEWS

Amidst the pine trees on the Aventine hill, which offers a spectacular view of the city, you'll find the gorgeous Giardino degli Aranci (garden of the orange trees).

When the weather is nice – in other words, very often – singers regularly come here at sunset to croon old Italian tunes to the great delight of everyone present.

DAILY: from sunrise to sunset

TALKING TO ANGELS
IN THE BASILICA OF
SANTI QUATTRO CORONATI

Far from the usual tourist routes, in the district of Celio, the fortified Basilica of Santi Quattro Coronati is one of the most charming churches in Rome.

We recommend visiting the church shortly before closing time to attend vespers sung by the nuns who live in the adjacent convent. In an atmosphere marked by deep contemplation, their voices echo below the vaults of the church and bring a real sense of peace.

Take a moment to admire the magnificent floor that underwent reconstruction work during the 11th century and is made of marble from the Roman Forums.

Before vespers, be sure to visit the monastery and admire the beautiful frescoes in the Chapel of St Sylvester. The wonderful cloister opens onto the nuns' chambers.

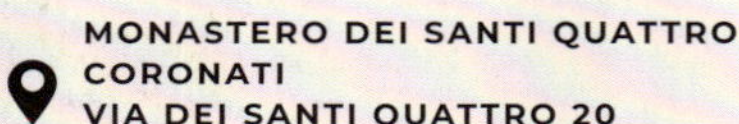

MONASTERO DEI SANTI QUATTRO CORONATI
VIA DEI SANTI QUATTRO 20

+39 06 7047 5427

monachess4@gmail.com

Chapel of St Sylvester: accessible from the second courtyard on the right. Use the bell of the convent's anteroom

GO FOR A RIDE
ON THE OLDEST ROAD IN THE WORLD

A 20-minute car ride from the city centre, at the corner of Via Cecilia Metella, Caffè Appia Antica is where you should go to rent a bike or a horse to explore a section of the magnificent Via Appia, the oldest paved road in the world. Roam the Roman countryside on thousand-year-old lava-stone paving amidst villas and the ruins of gravestones that still slumber between the pine and cypress trees.

Give it a go on a Sunday, when the Appian Way is closed to cars.

 **APPIA ANTICA CAFFÈ BICI E CAVALLI**
VIA APPIA ANTICA 175

+39 06 8987 9575 (landline) / +39 375 504 6930 (mobile)
info@appiaanticacaffe.it
appiaanticacaffe.it

To rent a horse, give Roberto a call:
+39 348 446 4094 (mobile)

THE BEST PIZZA
IN ROME

The 'Pizza Awards 2019' proclaimed Pier Daniele Seu the best *pizzaiolo* in Rome – and the eighth best in all of Italy. Far from offering the classic *margherita* or four-cheese pizza, Pier Daniele has set himself apart by venturing off the beaten track. Nothing is run of the mill at Seu Pizza Illuminati – especially not the pizza, which features a puffed outer crust (called *canotto* by the Neapolitans), a far cry from the Roman tradition which favours a very thin crust.

So head over to this inconspicuous little street in Trastevere to try the *'fior di cotto'* pizza (squash blossoms, cream, *stracciatella* cheese, cooked ham, seawater and olive powder) or the vegetarian *'Basilicata* coast to coast'.

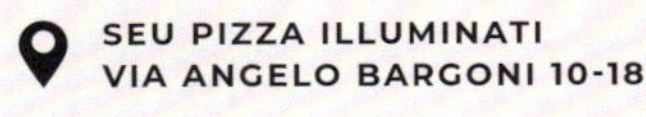

SEU PIZZA ILLUMINATI
VIA ANGELO BARGONI 10-18

+39 06 588 3384

seupizza.com

in pizza we trust

'PIZZA IS LOVE ...'

As Pier Daniele Seu puts it, 'For me, pizza is love, colour and poetry. LOVE because it's an unconditional feeling; in Italian it rhymes with sweetness, passion and creation. It's giving your time and energy to create something that touches someone else with every bite. COLOUR because my vision of pizza takes aesthetics into account. I enjoy inventing combinations that always feature a complex array of toppings. POETRY because I play with nature and its protagonists. The ingredients should give each pizza its own distinct rhymes.'

VISIT ONE OF ROME'S MOST MAGICAL PLACES
WITHOUT THE CROWDS

The Baths of Caracalla are undoubtedly one of the most exceptional places to visit in Rome.

The spectacular dimensions of these ancient Roman public baths, the many preserved and restored mosaic floors, the absence of the usual tourist crowds, and the new 'water mirror' that majestically reflects part of the ruins – all combine to make it one of the most enchanting places in the city.

As you leave, you might find your thoughts drifting to the idea of a wealthy investor recreating these baths in today's Rome …

An absolute must-see, even if it's your first time in the Eternal City.

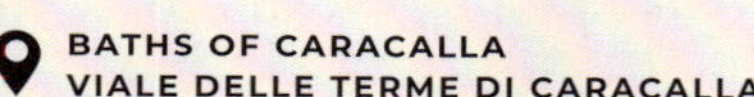

BATHS OF CARACALLA
VIALE DELLE TERME DI CARACALLA 52

soprintendenzaspecialeroma.it   ss-abap-rm@cultura.gov.it

A BISCUIT THAT WILL
TAKE YOU BACK
IN TIME

In a quiet corner of Trastevere, Biscottificio Artigiano Innocenti produces traditional biscuits in a delightful bakery designed around its superb 1950s oven. To go on a nostalgic trip back in time, just push open the doors to this shop run by Stefania, a fourth-generation member of the founding family.

Be sure to try one of their star biscuits: the *brutti ma buoni* ('ugly but good').

 **BISCOTTIFICIO ARTIGIANO INNOCENTI**
VIA DELLA LUCE 21

+39 06 580 3926

biscottificioartigianoinnocenti.wordpress.com
biscottificioinnocenti@gmail.com

QUI NON SI USANO GRASSI ANIMALI !

Il Dolce Servizo
Tel 0683...
info...
MULINO A PIETRA NATURALE
DELLA LANGA
MARINO

LIKE A SUNDAY
IN THE COUNTRY

At the heart of the magnificent gardens of the Villa Doria Pamphili, 10 minutes south of central Rome by car, Vivi Bistrot has, ever since it opened, been offering ready-to-go picnic baskets. Pick one up at the restaurant and set out into the huge park on foot or by bike to enjoy lunch al fresco – like a Sunday in the country. Brilliant.

If you prefer not to wander so far, the terrace in the garden is superb. At night, enjoy a candlelit dinner in a former barn in the park.

PHOTO CREDIT: SAGHAR SETAREH

VIVI BISTROT
VILLA DORIA PAMPHILJ
VIA VITELLIA 102

+39 06 582 7540

vivi.it/store/villa-pamphili

VIVI
BISTROT

A GREAT LITTLE BISTRO
IN A FISHMONGER'S SHOP

Located about ten minutes by car from Rome's historic centre, Meglio Fresco (meaning 'better fresh') is a delightful fishmonger's shop that transforms itself into a fantastic fish and seafood restaurant at lunch and dinner time.

Once the shutters of the shop have been lowered, the owners Arturo and Mary set up a few tables next to the display of the catch of the day. Here you can savour specialities like broccoli and skate soup, spaghetti with sea urchins, and Catalan-style lobster, all of it washed down with excellent wine.

A moment of true joy ...

MEGLIO FRESCO

Roma Boccea
Via di Boccea 350/A
+39 06 663 5411

Roma Vigna Clara
Via Pompeo Neri 42
+39 06 3974 4119

megliofresco.it

Mercato fresco
fresco
48.00

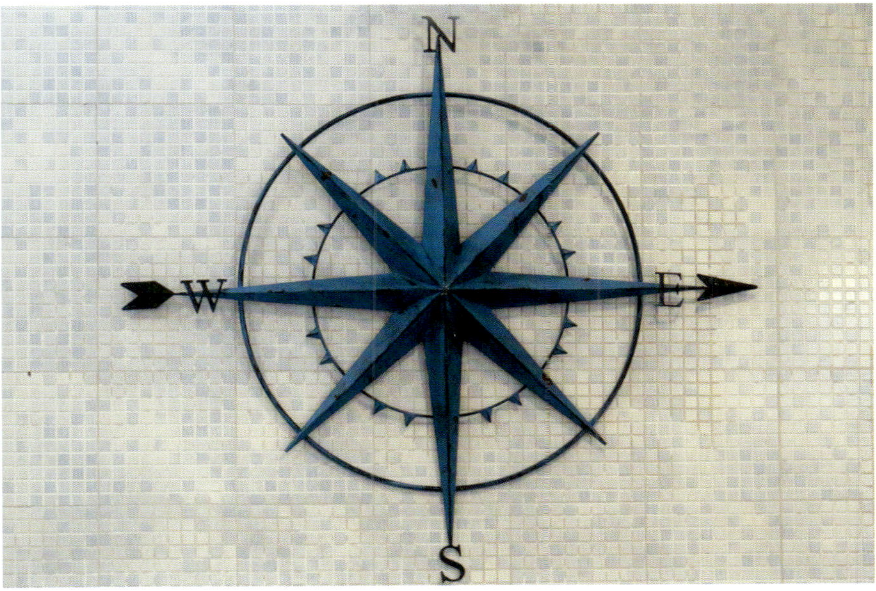

N
W
E
S

- FULVIO PIERANGELINI -

PERFECTION MADE SIMPLE

After earning every star and charming every critic, Fulvio Pierangelini, Italy's best chef (yes, you read that right: best chef) closed his restaurant to travel around the world and helm the kitchens of the Rocco Forte Hotels group. Now, still basking in his exceptional reputation, he's back in Rome, where he runs the kitchens at Hotel de la Ville, after having taken charge of those at Hotel de Russie.

Fulvio, your cooking smells deliciously of jasmine and oranges. But what's the flavour of Rome?

Rome teaches the art of seduction. You learn about the flavours of its markets, countless leaves, herbs that allow you to make apparently simple everyday – sometimes even banal – dishes, but which should be made with the very feminine instinct of trusting one's senses. I'd say above all, an obsessive attention to ingredients.

What does being born in Rome and having studied political sciences mean to you?

While I may be Roman on the one hand, and consequently the child of multiple and complex cultural strata, on the other, I look for perfection in simplicity and openness towards the rest of the world.

I didn't travel for decades; I was afraid of flying. Today I'm constantly on the go. I'm still anchored in pasta with tomato sauce, the Parmesan in *parmigiana*, and veal *tonnato*, but I also play with Middle Eastern spices.

Do you have any culinary taboos?

I don't like the banality of contemporary cuisine that feels it has to '*épater le bourgeois*' (shock the middle class) by aspiring to pointless excess. I hate terms like 'deconstructed', 'revamped' and 'gourmet'. I try to keep things simple and follow the compass of what's 'good', whether I'm cooking privately for the VIPs of the world or sharing my recipes in the places I host.

How would you describe yourself?

Dynamic, erratic, strict

MOSAICO 
Via Sistina, 69
+39 06 9779 3710
Daily for breakfast, lunch and dinner,
on the second floor of the Hotel de la Ville
(enter through the hotel courtyard
or banquet hall)

DA SISTINA 
Via Sistina, 39
+39 06 9779 3710
Daily

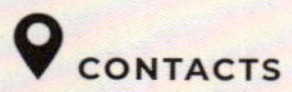

VISITING THE VATICAN
WITHOUT TOURISTS

While there's no doubt that the Vatican Museums are fabulous, visiting them at the same time as everyone else, drowned in masses of tourists, can ruin the experience.

To visit these magical spaces in the peace and quiet they deserve, just put yourself in the hands of an expert guide, who will let you in before the doors open to the public in a group of six to eight people at most (or even for a private tour, depending on your budget …).

For the even greater privilege of discovering rooms that are usually closed to the public, ask your guide to make a reservation to visit the Gabinetto delle Maschere or the Sala degli Animali. That's as much as we'll say.

📍 **CONTACTS**

Carolina Vincenti: cvincenti@inwind.it
(Italian, English and French)
Francesca Corsi: francescacorsi@yahoo.com
(Italian, English and French)

Paola Lauro : paolalauro@tiscali.it
(Italian, English and French)

MVSEI VATICANI

THE PRIVILEGE OF VISITING
ROME'S MOST PRIVATE VILLA

Contrary to what many people – even some Romans – think, you *can* visit the exceptional Villa Albani Torlonia not far from the Galleria Borghese. Just go to the foundation's website, download the request form, agree to pay 50 euros per person and then cross your fingers.

The foundation may contact you to offer a guided tour led by an art historian, with a group of twenty participants (English translation is available). Thanks to these tours, which usually take place on Fridays or Saturdays at 3pm, you'll have the privilege of visiting the villa, built between 1747 and 1767 for Cardinal Alessandro Albani, nephew of Pope Clement XI, and bought by the Torlonia family in 1867.

VILLA ALBANI TORLONIA
VIA SALARIA 92

fondazionetorlonia.org/visiting

The villa complex was designed by a host of painters, anti-
quarians, sculptors and architects, led by Winckelmann, Mengs,
Piranesi and Thorvaldsen, with the aim of encouraging a love
of antiquity, initiating the classicist movement that would soon
dominate Europe. Refined in both spirit and stone, the villa
never became a home, and remains a museum of classical
beauty to this day.

HPINNH

BIBLIOTECA ANGELICA

ROME'S
LOVELIEST
LIBRARIES

When visiting Rome, people often forget to explore its libraries. Which is such a pity, as the city boasts some of the loveliest libraries in the world. Few tourists know about most of them, which just adds to the appeal of discovering them.

> The **Biblioteca Angelica** is the oldest library in Rome (1604). This precious collection of old books was named Angelica in honour of Angelo Rocca, who bequeathed it to the Augustinian convent in 1604. Guided tours are offered, and concerts and exhibitions are held here regularly.

BIBLIOTECA ANGELICA
PIAZZA DI SANT'AGOSTINO 8

+39 06 684 0801   bibliotecaangelica.cultura.gov.it

BIBLIOTECA ALESSANDRINA

BIBLIOTECA VALLICELLIANA

COLLEGIO ROMANO

> The **Biblioteca Vallicelliana**, on the second floor of the Oratorio dei Filippini (Oratory of St Philip Neri, who was its founder – see our other guide, *Secret Rome*), was established in the 17th century. Don't forget to look for the opening in the floor of the library, which allowed students at the time to listen to the sacred music being played in the oratory below. The large reading room, which is still open at the top of a dramatic staircase, was designed by the melancholy Francesco Borromini.

> The ***Sala della Crociera*** and **Reading Room in the Roman College**: even many Romans don't know about these beautiful spaces dating from the 17th century.

> The **Biblioteca Casanatense**, founded in 1701 near the Dominican convent adjoining the Church of Santa Maria sopra Minerva on Piazza della Minerva, holds a large collection of legal, theological and philosophical texts.

> The spectacular **Biblioteca Alessandrina** in the Palazzo della Sapienza, at the entrance to the famous Church of Sant'Ivo alla Sapienza (designed by Borromini), was founded in the 17th century.

<table>
<tr><td>📍 BIBLIOTECA VALLICELLIANA
PIAZZA DELLA CHIESA NUOVA 18</td><td>📍 COLLEGIO ROMANO
PIAZZA DEL COLLEGIO ROMANO 1/A</td></tr>
<tr><td>vallicelliana.cultura.gov.it</td><td>vive.cultura.gov.it</td></tr>
<tr><td>📍 BIBLIOTECA CASANATENSE
VIA DI SANT'IGNAZIO 52</td><td>📍 BIBLIOTECA ALESSANDRINA
PIAZZALE ALDO MORO 5</td></tr>
<tr><td>casanatense.cultura.gov.it</td><td>alessandrina.cultura.gov.it</td></tr>
</table>

BIBLIOTECA CASANATENSE

JOGGING AMONG THE
GODS OF THE STADIUM

After strolling around the Vatican Museums for hours, sometimes you're in the mood for some real sport. To go for a jog in beautiful surroundings, head over to the magnificent Stadio dei Marmi ('marble stadium'), where you can step up your pace while admiring the 64 statues dedicated to athletes that will transform a simple stroll into a theatrical experience.

Designed as the Foro Mussolini in 1928 and inaugurated in 1932 to celebrate the spirit of competition under the Fascist regime, the stadium overlooks the immaculate green of Monte Mario, the imposing mass of the 1930s-style Ministry of Foreign Affairs and, in the distance, the waters of the Tiber. *Mens sana in corpore sano* – with the added bonus of some breathtaking views.

Two other good places to go jogging near the historic centre: around the Circus Maximus and along the banks of the Tiber.

 **VIALE DELLO STADIO DEI MARMI**

+39 06 324 0334 +39 331 946 7228	marmi@fidallazio.it	Free admission

VISIT ONE OF THE MOST BEAUTIFUL VILLAS IN ITALY

Rome is full of so many wonderful treasures that it wouldn't necessarily occur to you to leave the city if you re only there for a couple of days. And yet, escaping the hustle and bustle and the crowds of tourists to discover the surrounding areas of the capital is a real treat, especially if the programme includes the fabulous Villa Farnese in the small village of Caprarola, just an hour from Rome.

Built during the Renaissance by the Farnese family, the villa (officially called the Palazzo Farnese di Caprarola) is without a doubt one of the most beautiful in the whole of Italy. Its monumental staircase (the Scala Regia) and the Room of Maps (Sala del Mappamondo by Giovanni Antonio ca Varese, nicknamed the Venosino) are absolute masterpieces that would rank as the highlights of any visit.

Another great advantage of the villa is that, along with its beautiful Italian gardens, it is virtually unknown to tourists, so you can expect to be practically alone there!

VILLA FARNESE
PIAZZA FARNESE 1
01032 CAPRAROLA VT

visitcaprarola.it/fr/luoghi-da-visitare/edifici-storici/pa azzo-farnese

Many thanks to Paolo Scotto di Castelbianco for sharing his deep knowledge of Rome.

This book was created by:

Carolina Vincenti, author

Sofia Bernardini and Claire de Virieu, photographers

Clara Mari, illustrator

Emmanuelle Willard Toulemonde, layout

Sophie Schlondorff, translation

Jana Gough, editing

Kimberly Bess and Caroline Lawrence, proofreading

Clémence Mathé, Roberto Sassi and Morgane De Wulf, publishing

You can write to us at info@editionsjonglez.com

Follow us on Instagram: @editionsjonglez

THANK YOU

From the same publisher

Atlases

Atlas of extreme weather
Atlas of forbidden places
Atlas of geographical curiosities
Atlas of unusual wines

Photo Books

Abandoned America
Abandoned Asylums
Abandoned Australia
Abandoned Belgium
Abandoned Churches: Unclaimed places of worship
Abandoned cinemas of the world
Abandoned France
Abandoned Germany
Abandoned Italy
Abandoned Japan
Abandoned Lebanon
Abandoned Spain
Abandoned USSR
Abandoned world – An AI-generated exploration
After the Final Curtain – The Fall of the American Movie Theater
After the Final Curtain – America's Abandoned Theaters
Baikonur – Vestiges of the Soviet space programme
Cinemas – A French heritage
Clickbait – A visual journey through AI-generated stories
Destination Wellness – The 35 best places in the world to take time out
Forbidden France
Forbidden Places – Vol. 1
Forbidden Places – Vol. 2
Forbidden Places – Vol. 3
Forgotten Heritage
Oblivion
Secret sacred sites
Venice deserted
Venice from the skies

'Soul of' Guides

Soul of Amsterdam
Soul of Athens
Soul of Barcelona
Soul of Berlin
Soul of Brussels
Soul of Kyoto
Soul of Lisbon
Soul of Los Angeles
Soul of Marrakesh
Soul of Marseille
Soul of Milan
Soul of New York
Soul of Paris
Soul of Tokyo
Soul of Venice

'Secret' Guides

Follow us on Facebook and Instagram

Cover photo: © Marialaura Gionfriddo – Unsplash
4th cover designed by Freepik

© JONGLEZ 2025
Registration of copyright: March 2025 - Edition: 03
ISBN: 978-2-36195-858-9
Printed in Slovakia by Polygraf